THE PRESIDENTS' LITTLE INSTRUCTION BOOK

The Presidents' Little Instruction Book
ISBN 1-57757-008-1
Copyright © 1996 by Trade Life Books, Inc.
P. O. Box 55325
Tulsa, Oklahoma 74155

INTRODUCTION

They are the men who have led our country in its fight for freedom. Some ingenious. Some reserved. Some outrageous! All of them ordinary men who became extraordinary.

What can we learn from these men of destiny? What words of wisdom do they leave for us today?

The Presidents' Little Instruction Book presents the dynamic viewpoints and distinct uniqueness of each American President who, in the tumult of their times, were elevated to the highest office in the land!

Learn *from* them! Learn *about* them!

The Presidents' Little Instruction Book is a legacy time capsule. *You'll never view history the same again!*

GEORGE WASHINGTON, FEDERALIST
1st President: 1789-1797
Vice-President: John Adams

★ ★ ★

Born:	February 22, 1732; Virginia
Occupation:	Plantation owner, Soldier
Wife:	Martha Custis
Children:	Two stepchildren, two adopted children
Died:	December 14, 1799
Buried:	Mount Vernon, Virginia

★ ★ ★

Notable facts: U.S. courts organized; Bill of Rights ratified.

Never more truly at his best than in situations which were seemingly hopeless. Remembered as the "Father of His Country."

George Washington

*Few men have virtue to withstand
the highest bidder.*

---

*Associate yourself with men of good quality
if you esteem your own reputation,
for 'tis better to be alone
than in bad company.*

GEORGE WASHINGTON

*Be courteous to all, but intimate with few,
and let those few be well tried before
you give them your confidence.*

---

*We ought not to look back unless
it is to derive useful lessons
from past errors. . . .*

DID YOU KNOW?

George Washington was offered a third term, but refused it believing that two terms was as long as any one person should serve. This set a precedent which was not broken until 1940 when Franklin Roosevelt was re-elected for a third term. Soon after Roosevelt's reign an amendment was established supporting the standard of Washington allowing only two terms.

JOHN ADAMS, FEDERALIST
2nd President: 1797-1801
Vice-President: Thomas Jefferson

★ ★ ★

Born:	October 30, 1735; Massachusetts
Occupation:	Lawyer, Diplomat
Wife:	Abigail Smith
Children:	Three sons, two daughters
Died:	July 4, 1826
Buried:	Quincy, Massachusetts

★ ★ ★

Notable facts: Responsible for George Washington's appointment
as Commander-in-Chief; conferred the writing of
the Declaration of Independence upon Jefferson;
Navy Department created during term.

In every station, displayed brilliance, talent and virtue.

John Adams

*There is nothing so likely to produce peace
as to be well prepared to meet an enemy.*

---

*Liberty . . . is an intellectual quality.
Let the human mind loose.*

John Adams

The preservation of the means of knowledge among the lowest ranks is of more importance to the public than all the property of all the rich men in the country.

DID YOU KNOW?

Abigail Adams, wife of John Adams, was the only woman to be wife of one President and mother of another—John Quincy Adams.

Thomas Jefferson, Democratic-Republican

3rd President: 1801-1809
Vice-Presidents: Aaron Burr, George Clinton

★ ★ ★

Born:	April 13, 1743; Virginia
Occupation:	Lawyer, Farmer
Wife:	Martha Skelton
Children:	One son, five daughters
Died:	July 4, 1826
Buried:	Monticello, Virginia

★ ★ ★

Notable facts: Authored Declaration of Independence; Louisiana Purchase added immense territory to U.S. during his term.

Considered the greatest architect of his time, it was impossible for him to look at a thing without wanting to improve it.

THOMAS JEFFERSON

No man has a natural right to commit aggression on the equal rights of another.

---

*Whenever you are to do a thing . . .
ask yourself how you would act
were all the world looking at you,
and act accordingly.*

THOMAS JEFFERSON

That government is best which governs the least, because its people discipline themselves.

DID YOU KNOW?

Thomas Jefferson exerted his influence through prolific writing of letters and articles, which he was known to write standing up!

JAMES MADISON, DEMOCRATIC-REPUBLICAN
4th President: 1809-1817
Vice-Presidents: George Clinton, Elbridge Gerry

Born:	March 16, 1751; Virginia
Occupation:	Plantation owner, Statesman, Lawyer
Wife:	Dorothea Payne Todd
Children:	One stepchild
Died:	June 28, 1836
Buried:	Montpelier, Virginia

Notable facts: National Road begun; War of 1812 fought between U.S. and Great Britain.

A strong promoter of privacy and individual rights, thus at times condemned as an "elitist."

Remembered as the "Father of the Constitution."

James Madison

The diffusion of knowledge is the only guardian of true liberty.

In all cases where the majority are united by a common interest or passion, the rights of the minority are in danger.

JAMES MADISON

The religion . . . of every man must be left to the conviction and conscience of every man.

James Madison, at 5'4" and weighing 100 pounds, was both the smallest President and the first sitting President to serve actively in the field under gunfire as Commander-in-Chief of the U.S. Armed Forces.

JAMES MONROE, DEMOCRATIC-REPUBLICAN
5th President: 1817-1825
Vice-President: Daniel D. Tompkins

★ ★ ★

Born: April 28, 1758; Virginia
Occupation: Lawyer
Wife: Elizabeth Kortwright
Children: Two daughters
Died: July 4, 1831
Buried: Richmond, Virginia

★ ★ ★

Notable facts: Presided over "The Era of Good Feelings"; first public high school opened; Monroe Doctrine proclaimed, setting distinct political boundaries between Western Hemisphere and European powers; treaty signed settling Canadian boundary.

Unlike his presidential predecessors, he always *wanted* to be in politics.

JAMES MONROE

In this great nation there is but one order, that of the people . . . .

Our great resources . . . are more especially to be found in the virtue, patriotism and intelligence of our fellow-citizens . . . .

James Monroe dropped out of college to join Washington's army, later studied law under Thomas Jefferson, held more political offices than any other President, and was the last of the Revolutionary leaders to become President.

James Monroe is the young man depicted holding the flag in the famous painting, "Washington Crossing the Delaware."

JOHN QUINCY ADAMS, DEMOCRATIC-REPUBLICAN
6th President: 1825-1829
Vice-President: John C. Calhoun

Born:	July 11, 1767; Massachusetts
Occupation:	Lawyer, Statesman
Wife:	Louisa Catherine Johnson
Children:	Three sons, one daughter
Died:	February 23, 1848
Buried:	Quincy, Massachusetts

Notable facts: Erie Canal opened.

Only son of a President to become President!

John Quincy Adams

To furnish the means of acquiring knowledge is . . . the greatest benefit that can be conferred upon mankind.

Women exhibit the most exalted virtue when they depart from the domestic circle and enter on the concerns of their country, of humanity, and of their God!

JOHN QUINCY ADAMS

Individual liberty is individual power.

John Quincy Adams loved to "skinny dip" in the Potomac River in the early hours of warm days during his presidency!

ANDREW JACKSON, DEMOCRAT

7th President: 1829-1837

Vice-Presidents: John C. Calhoun, Martin Van Buren

★ ★ ★

Born:	March 15, 1767, South Carolina
Occupation:	Lawyer, General
Wife:	Rachel Robards
Children:	One son, adopted
Died:	June 8, 1845
Buried:	The Hermitage, near Nashville, Tennessee

★ ★ ★

Notable facts: First nominating conventions held; Texas declared its independence.

Rough and rugged frontiersman known for fighting Indians and duels; named "Old Hickory" by the common people whose rights he championed, fighting for them against corruption; elected as a "man of the common people."

Andrew Jackson

The brave man inattentive to his duty is worth little more to his country than the coward who deserts her in the hour of danger.

I cannot be intimidated from doing that which my judgment and conscience tell me is right by any earthly power.

DID YOU KNOW?

 B orn on a ship bound for America from Ireland, and not on American soil, Andrew Jackson, according to the law, was "ineligible" for the Presidency, most likely making him an "illegal" President!

On Andrew Jackson's Inauguration Day in 1829, twenty *thousand* cheering Jackson fans jammed the White House, standing on chairs with muddy boots and spilling punch on the rugs, rendering the White House a filthy shambles.

Martin Van Buren, Democrat

8th President: 1837-1841
Vice-President: Richard M. Johnson

Born: December 5, 1782; New York
Occupation: Lawyer
Wife: Hannah Hoes
Children: Four sons
Died: July 24, 1862
Buried: Kinderhook, New York

Notable facts: Nation plunged into economic depression, ending Jacksonian era.

Believed that government was best which governed least; referred to as the "little magician" or "sly fox," he skillfully pitted faction against faction, molding consensus toward his own ends; a true "father of modern political science."

DID YOU KNOW ?

Martin Van Buren also served as New York State Senator, United States Senator, Governor of New York, and Secretary of State and Vice-President during Jackson's terms, but was known to habitually sleep until noon!

WILLIAM HENRY HARRISON, WHIG
9th President: 1841, served only one month
Vice-President: John Tyler

★ ★ ★

Born:	February 9, 1773; Virginia
Occupation:	Farmer, Soldier
Wife:	Anna Symmes
Children:	Six sons, five daughters
Died:	April 4, 1841
Buried:	North Bend, Ohio

★ ★ ★

Notable facts: National hero for leading and winning battle at Tippecanoe River, making famous his presidential political slogan, "Tippecanoe and Tyler, too!"; died thirty-two days after taking office.

William Henry Harrison

The only legitimate right to govern is an express grant of power from the governed.

The strongest of all governments is that which is most free.

DID YOU KNOW?

William Henry Harrison at age 68 was the oldest man to be elected President up till that time. On a cold and rainy Inauguration Day, to show his good health, he refused to wear an overcoat. Subsequently, he contracted pneumonia and died just one month after taking office. As a result, he became the first President to die in office and is the President who has served the shortest term in office.

William Henry Harrison was the youngest child born to Benjamin Harrison, one of the signers of the Declaration of Independence, and was grandfather to Benjamin Harrison, America's 23rd President.

JOHN TYLER, WHIG
10th President: 1841-1845
Vice-President: Samuel L. Southard, Senate President pro tempore

★ ★ ★

Born: March 29, 1790; Virginia
Occupation: Lawyer
Wives: Letitia Christian, Julia Gardiner
Children: Eight sons, seven daughters
Died: January 17, 1862
Buried: Richmond, Virginia

★ ★ ★

Notable facts: Clarified, solidified Vice-President's "right of presidential succession," complete with full presidential pow-
ers; first time labor unions given legal recognition.

Known widely as "the President without a party."

John Tyler

*Wealth can only be accumulated by the earnings
of industry and the savings of frugality.*

---

*The great primary and controlling interest
of the American people is union . . .
union founded in an attachment of . . .
individuals for each other.*

JAMES K. POLK, DEMOCRAT
11th President: 1845-1849
Vice-President: George M. Dallas

★ ★ ★

Born:	November 2, 1795; North Carolina
Occupation:	Lawyer
Wife:	Sarah Childress
Children:	None
Died:	June 15, 1849
Buried:	Nashville, Tennessee

★ ★ ★

Notable facts: Vast expansion of American territory, acquiring entire Southwest and far West during a single term; first women's rights convention.

First little-known or "dark horse" candidate to reach the White House.

James K. Polk, a "workaholic" President, worked so hard at being a good President, that he did everything himself rather than trusting anything to his aides. He rose at daybreak, worked until midnight, then recorded into the wee hours the details of the day in his diary. As a result, Polk became worn out from his hard work, did not seek a second term, and unfortunately died three months after leaving office.

ZACHARY TAYLOR, WHIG
12th President: 1849-1850
Vice-President: Millard Fillmore

★ ★ ★

Born: November 24, 1784; Virginia
Occupation: Military Officer
Wife: Margaret Smith
Children: One son, five daughters
Died: July 9, 1850
Buried: Louisville, Kentucky

★ ★ ★

Notable facts: California gold rush took place.

Became prominent national hero, winning victory over Mexican leader Santa Anna, battle of Buena Vista; dubbed affectionately "Old Rough and Ready" by his troops because of his slovenly dress.

Before being nominated by the Whig party, Zachary Taylor was known to avoid politics and politicians, had never in his life cast a vote in a presidential election, resisted the nomination, refused to campaign, yet still won the election.

MILLARD FILLMORE, WHIG
13th President: 1850-1853

Vice-Presidents: Howell Cobb, Speaker of the House;
William R. D. King, David R. Atchison,
Presidents pro tempore of the Senate

★ ★ ★

Born: January 7, 1800, New York
Occupation: Lawyer
Wives: Abigail Powers, Caroline McIntosh
Children: One son, one daughter
Died: March 8, 1874
Buried: Buffalo, New York

★ ★ ★

Notable facts: An avid book lover, amassing a personal library of
over four thousand volumes; establishing the first
White House Library; founded first public school
system, University of Buffalo, Buffalo General
Hospital, and Buffalo Fine Arts Academy.

MILLARD FILLMORE

The man who can look upon a crisis without being willing to offer himself upon the altar of his country is not fit for public trust.

An honorable defeat is better than a dishonorable victory.

MILLARD FILLMORE

Revolutions do not always establish freedom.

DID YOU KNOW?

Millard Fillmore first attended school at age eighteen, surrounded by seven- and eight-year-olds. Embarrassed, he nonetheless studied diligently, excelled and seven years later married his school-teacher. By his mid-forties, he had become a wealthy man earning more than $100,000 per year in his law practice.

FRANKLIN PIERCE, DEMOCRAT
14th President: 1853-1857
Vice-President: William R. King

★ ★ ★

Born:	November 23, 1804; New Hampshire
Occupation:	Lawyer
Wife:	Jane Appleton
Children:	Three sons
Died:	October 8, 1869
Buried:	Concord, New Hampshire

★ ★ ★

Notable facts: Republican party formed, anti-slavery platform developed; violated Missouri Compromise by passing Kansas-Nebraska Act of 1854, resulting in territory known as "Bleeding Kansas," the determining factor in the development of the North-South split.

DID YOU KNOW?

Franklin Pierce's best friends were Nathaniel Hawthorne and Henry Wadsworth Longfellow.

JAMES BUCHANAN, DEMOCRAT
15th President: 1857-1861
Vice-President: John C. Breckenridge

Born:	April 23, 1791; Pennsylvania
Occupation:	Lawyer
Wife:	None
Children:	None
Died:	June 1, 1868
Buried:	Lancaster, Pennsylvania

Notable facts: Slavery emerged as the one, all-encompassing issue —
prompting loss of re-election to Abraham Lincoln; Con-
federacy formed.

Heartbroken as a young man with the death of his fiancé, he
vowed to never marry; a vow he kept. Thus he became the
only bachelor to occupy the White House and his orphaned
niece took the role behind his personal and political success.

JAMES BUCHANAN

Liberty must be allowed to work out its natural results; and these will . . . astonish the world.

There is nothing stable but Heaven and the Constitution.

Abraham Lincoln, Republican
16th President: 1861-1865
Vice-Presidents: Hannibal Hamlin, Andrew Johnson

★ ★ ★

Born: February 12, 1809; Kentucky
Occupation: Lawyer
Wife: Mary Todd
Children: Four sons
Died: April 15, 1865
Buried: Springfield, Illinois

★ ★ ★

Notable facts: The Lincoln-Douglas Debates regarding slavery; Gettysburg Address; beginning and end of the Civil War; Emancipation Proclamation, ending slavery; assassinated.

Great not only in what he did, but in how he did it —loving mankind, demonstrating his belief in true justice for all.

ABRAHAM LINCOLN

Truth is . . . the best vindication against slander.

To sin by silence when they should protest makes cowards of men.

Abraham Lincoln

A house divided against itself cannot stand.

Let us have faith that right makes might . . . .
Having thus chosen our course . . .
let us renew our trust in God and
go forward without fear . . . .

DID
YOU
KNOW
?

Abraham Lincoln once described his best friend as the man who could get him a book he hadn't yet read.

ANDREW JOHNSON, REPUBLICAN

17th President: 1865-1869

Vice-Presidents: Lafayette Sabine Foster, Benjamin Franklin Wade,
Presidents pro tempore of the Senate

★ ★ ★

Born:	December 29, 1808; North Carolina
Occupation:	Tailor, Military Governor, Statesman, Municipal Legislator
Wife:	Eliza McCardle
Children:	Three sons, two daughters
Died:	July 31, 1875
Buried:	Greeneville, Tennessee

★ ★ ★

Notable facts: Passage of Thirteenth Amendment abolishing slavery; Homestead Act, opening up vast, unsettled areas of the West; impeached by House, acquitted by Senate.

Andrew Johnson

Honest conviction is my courage . . . .

The goal to strive for is a poor government, but a rich people.

Andrew Johnson

*A sparing economy is itself
a great national resource.*

DID YOU KNOW?

Andrew Johnson was the only President at this point in American history to attain to all three branches of office—executive, legislative, and judicial—and yet he had no formal schooling. His wife taught him to read and write!

ULYSSES S. GRANT, REPUBLICAN

18th President: 1869-1877
Vice-Presidents: Schuyler Colfax, Henry Wilson

Born:	April 27, 1822; Ohio
Occupation:	General, Commander-in-Chief
Wife:	Julia B. Dent
Children:	Two sons, two daughters
Died:	July 23, 1885
Buried:	New York City

Notable facts: First transcontinental railroad completed.

Secured Lee's unconditional surrender at Appomattox, gaining him the nickname "Unconditional Surrender Grant"; a national hero after the Civil War, Congress appointed him a full General, the first to hold such rank since George Washington.

ULYSSES S. GRANT

*Social equality is not a subject
to be legislated upon.*

Labor disgraces no man.

Grant was scheduled to attend the Ford Theater with Abraham Lincoln on April 14, 1865. John Wilkes Booth, carrying a big knife, planned to use the knife on Grant after shooting Lincoln. Grant, however, altered his plans at the last minute to catch a train to see his children, a decision which most likely saved his life.

Ex-President Grant, knowing he was dying of throat cancer, never a good businessman, and fearing leaving his wife in debt and penniless, wrote a 1231-page, personal memoir upon his deathbed. Finishing it only three days before his death, the two-volume autobiography became a major bestseller, leaving his widow the huge sum of $450,000.

RUTHERFORD B. HAYES, REPUBLICAN
19th President: 1877-1881
Vice-President: William A. Wheeler

★ ★ ★

Born: October 4, 1822; Ohio
Occupation: Lawyer
Wife: Lucy Webb
Children: Seven sons, one daughter
Died: January 17, 1893
Buried: Fremont, Ohio

★ ★ ★

Notable facts: Withdrew last federal troops from South, ending
               Reconstruction.

               Restored dignity to White House after Grant's scandalous administration.

Rutherford B. Hayes

Sectionalism and race prejudice . . . are the only two enemies America has any cause to fear.

It is now true that this is God's Country, if equal rights—a fair start and an equal chance in the race of life are everywhere secured to all.

Rutherford B. Hayes was nominated for President the same month General Custer met his fate—June, 1876.

Rutherford Hayes' wife, Lucy, was the first "progressive" First Lady, having a college degree, supporting women's suffrage and Susan B. Anthony's national campaign to bring voting rights to women. As the women's-movement controversy stormed, Rutherford permitted his wife's activities and involvement, yet never publicly stated his position.

JAMES A. GARFIELD, REPUBLICAN
20th President: 1881, Six and one-half months
Vice-President: Chester A. Arthur

★ ★ ★

Born:	November 19, 1831; Ohio
Occupation:	Lawyer, General
Wife:	Lucretia Rudolph
Children:	Four sons, one daughter
Died:	September 19, 1881
Buried:	Cleveland, Ohio

★ ★ ★

Notable facts: American Red Cross founded.

Youngest brigadier general of Civil War; fourth President to die in office, assassinated in railway station, Washington, D.C.

James A. Garfield

I love . . . defending unpopular truth against popular error.

Justice and goodwill will outlast passion.

CHESTER A. ARTHUR, REPUBLICAN

21st President: 1881-1885

Vice-Presidents: Thomas F. Bayard, David Davis, George F. Edmunds,
Presidents pro tempore of the Senate

★ ★ ★

Born: October 5, 1830; Vermont
Occupation: Lawyer
Wife: Ellen Herndon
Children: Two sons, one daughter
Died: November 18, 1886
Buried: Albany, New York

★ ★ ★

Notable facts: Civil Service Commission established; Pendleton Act
passed, instituting modern civil service examinations.

Nicknamed "Elegant Arthur" for his lavish lifestyle,
spending two to three hours at the dinner table dining
on expensive wine and lavish meals prepared by his
French cook.

CHESTER A. ARTHUR

Men may die, but the fabrics of our free institutions remain unshaken.

If it were not for the reporters, I would tell you the truth!

(a statement he frustratedly made after many misrepresentations)

GROVER CLEVELAND, DEMOCRAT
22nd & 24th President: 1885-1889, 1893-1897
Vice-Presidents: Thomas A. Hendricks, Adlai E. Stevenson

Born:	March 18, 1837; New Jersey
Occupation:	Lawyer
Wife:	Frances Folsom
Children:	Two sons, three daughters
Died:	June 24, 1908
Buried:	Princeton, New Jersey

Notable facts: Division of Forestry created; first President to
marry actually in the White House.

Spoke out courageously and sensibly, without fear
to veto corruption.

Grover Cleveland

What is the use of being elected or re-elected, unless you stand for something?

A man is known by the company he keeps, and also by the company from which he is kept out.

Grover Cleveland authored eighteen articles for *The Saturday Evening Post* from 1901 to 1906—writing on topics ranging from politics to fish tales, publishing more articles than any other President before or since.

DID
YOU
KNOW
?

Grover Cleveland did not marry until he was forty-nine at which time his wife was twenty-one. Cleveland had been her guardian since she was eleven.

BENJAMIN HARRISON, REPUBLICAN
23rd President: 1889-1893
Vice-President: Levi P. Morton

★ ★ ★

Born:	August 20, 1833; Ohio
Occupation:	Lawyer
Wives:	Caroline Scott, Mary Scott Dimmick
Children:	One son, two daughters
Died:	March 13, 1901
Buried:	Indianapolis, Indiana

★ ★ ★

Notable facts: Sherman Antitrust Act, designed to destroy monopolies and restore competition; McKinley Tariff Act, highest protective tariff U.S. had seen up to that time; Dependent and Disability Pensions Act; end of the known frontier.

Grandson of ninth President. Known as one of the most reserved Presidents to hold office.

Benjamin Harrison

The manner by which women are treated is a good criterion to judge the true state of society.

I believe in the American opportunity which puts the starry sky above every boy's head, and sets his foot upon a ladder which he may climb until his strength gives out.

Benjamin Harrison was the first President to live with electric lights in the White House. However, the Harrisons were so fearful of the new device that they refused to touch the switches and would sleep through the night with all the lights on!

Harrison was both thorough and systematic, so much so that each day he worked all morning and spent all afternoon with his family, still completing his business at hand.

WILLIAM McKINLEY, REPUBLICAN
25th President: 1897-1901
Vice-Presidents: Garret A. Hobart, Theodore Roosevelt

★ ★ ★

Born:	January 29, 1843; Ohio
Occupation:	Lawyer
Wife:	Ida Saxton
Children:	Two daughters
Died:	September 14, 1901
Buried:	Canton, Ohio

★ ★ ★

Notable facts: Last Civil War veteran to become President; reconciled North and South by declaring the government would care for graves of the Confederate dead; Spanish-American War.

Considered frank, open, candid, kind, sincere. Much a man of the people; greatly mourned upon his assassination.

WILLIAM McKINLEY

In time of darkest defeat, victory may be nearest.

---

*All a man can hope for during his lifetime [is]
to set an example—and when he is dead,
to be an inspiration to history.*

WILLIAM McKINLEY

War should never be entered upon until every agency of peace has failed.

Our differences are policies, our agreements principles.

William McKinley, deeply devoted to his epileptic wife, determined never to leave her day or night. During a seizure he would gently tend to her. Once the seizure had passed, he would gently pat her on the cheek, fasten her shawl around her shoulders, then return to the business at hand as if nothing had happened.

THEODORE ROOSEVELT, REPUBLICAN
26th President: 1901-1909
Vice-President: John M. Hay

Born:	October 27, 1858; New York City
Occupation:	Navy Officer, Lawyer, President of NY Police Board, Governor
Wives:	Alice Lee, Edith Carow
Children:	Four sons, two daughters
Died:	January 6, 1919
Buried:	Oyster Bay, New York

Notable facts: Acquired Panama Canal Zone; built Panama Canal; promoted "square deal" for everyone.

Became a popular national hero during Spanish-American War by serving as the Lieutenant Colonel of the first U.S. volunteer cavalry regiment—the famous "Rough Riders".

THEODORE "TEDDY" ROOSEVELT

The first requisite of a good citizen . . .
is that he shall be able and
willing to pull his weight.

Actions speak louder than words.
Speak softly and carry a big stick.

Theodore Roosevelt, tenderhearted toward animals, was depicted in a cartoon by The Washington Post in which he refused to shoot a bear cub. The cartoon inspired the popular term used today: the "teddy bear."

After drinking his first cup of Maxwell House coffee, Teddy Roosevelt remarked, "Good to the last drop"—a remark which caught on and is still heard in American households today.

WILLIAM H. TAFT, REPUBLICAN
27th President: 1909-1913
Vice-President: James S. Sherman

★ ★ ★

Born: September 15, 1857; Ohio
Occupation: Lawyer
Wife: Helen Herron
Children: Two sons, one daughter
Died: March 8, 1930
Buried: Arlington National Cemetery

★ ★ ★

Notable facts: First state minimum-wage law; recommended Six-
teenth Amendment establishing federal income tax.

Known as "Big Bill," a large, jovial, easy-going man
standing six feet, two inches tall, weighing 332 pounds.

William H. Taft

Next to the right of liberty, the right of property is the most important individual right guaranteed by the Constitution . . . .

To resort to violence is out of place in our twentieth-century civilization.

DID YOU KNOW?

William Taft got stuck in the White House bathtub and a new tub was installed to fit him—a tub large enough to hold four ordinary men.

Taft disliked the Presidency, his lifelong dream always to be a Supreme Court justice—a dream fulfilled in 1921, resulting in nine years of service on the bench and a prolific 253 opinions.

WOODROW WILSON, DEMOCRAT
28th President: 1913-1921
Vice-President: Thomas R. Marshall

★ ★ ★

Born:	December 28, 1856; Virginia
Occupation:	Educator, Lawyer
Wives:	Ellen Axson, Edith Galt
Children:	Three daughters
Died:	February 3, 1924
Buried:	Washington, D.C.

★ ★ ★

Notable facts: World War I took place; passage of Eighteenth Amendment, prohibition; passage of Nineteenth Amendment, women given the right to vote.

Introduced "New Freedom" program concerned with restoring rights of all people, against special privileges for a few.

Woodrow Wilson

*Life does not consist in thinking,
it consists in acting.*

---

*One cool judgment is worth a thousand
hasty counsels; the thing to do is to
supply light and not heat.*

Woodrow Wilson gave his whole adult life to the study of government, being one of the few Presidents to take office with a fully-formed political philosophy. Instead of frowning upon independent thought, he delighted in it.

U pon an intensive tour to promote the League of Nations, Wilson suffered a stroke from which he never fully recovered. During the last seventeen months of his Presidency, Wilson's wife effectively took over the Presidency, causing some members of Congress to protest, "We have a petticoat government!"

WARREN G. HARDING, REPUBLICAN
29th President: 1921-1923
Vice-President: Calvin Coolidge

★ ★ ★

Born:	November 2, 1865; Ohio
Occupation:	Newspaper business owner
Wife:	Florence DeWolfe
Children:	None
Died:	August 2, 1923
Buried:	Marion, Ohio

★ ★ ★

Notable facts: Physical preservation of U.S. Constitution; Bureau of the Budget created to balance federal budget; Veterans' Bureau created.

Won the election because the women's movement supported him with their historical first right to vote. Even so, his reputation was tarnished, though innocent himself, his administration was embroiled in scandal.

WARREN G. HARDING

There's good in everybody.

America's present need is not heroics but healing . . . .

Warren G. Harding once took employment as a school teacher but quit after one term saying it was the hardest job he ever had.

Harding was the first President to ride to his inauguration in an automobile and to have his inauguration broadcast over radio.

CALVIN COOLIDGE, REPUBLICAN
30th President: 1923-1929
Vice-President: Charles G. Dawes

★ ★ ★

Born:	July 4, 1872; Vermont
Occupation:	Lawyer
Wife:	Grace Goodhue
Children:	Two sons
Died:	January 5, 1933
Buried:	Plymouth, Vermont

★ ★ ★

Notable facts: All Indians given citizenship.

A man of few words, known to be honest and calm.
His thrifty nature restored the public's confidence
after the scandals of the previous administration.
Slogan of the day: "Keep cool with Coolidge."

CALVIN COOLIDGE

There is no dignity quite so impressive, and no independence quite so important, as living within your means.

No person was ever honored for what he received. Honor has been the reward for what he gave.

CALVIN COOLIDGE

If you don't say anything, you won't be called upon to repeat it.

Nothing I've never said has hurt me.

CALVIN COOLIDGE

Perhaps one of [my] most important accomplishments has been minding my own business.

HERBERT HOOVER, REPUBLICAN
31st President: 1929-1933
Vice-President: Charles Curtis

★ ★ ★

Born: August 10, 1874; West Branch, Iowa
Occupation: Engineer
Wife: Lou Henry
Children: Two sons
Died: October 20, 1964
Buried: West Branch, Iowa

★ ★ ★

Notable facts: Hoover Dam built; stock market crash of 1929 took place; Great Depression began.

First President born west of Mississippi River; mining engineer; multimillionaire.

HERBERT HOOVER

Progress of the nation is the sum of progress of its individuals.

Children are our most valuable natural resource.

HERBERT HOOVER

*No man can be just
a little crooked.*

HERBERT HOOVER

*Free speech does not live many hours
after free industry and
free commerce die.*

FRANKLIN D. ROOSEVELT, DEMOCRAT
32nd President: 1933-1945
Vice-Presidents: John N. Garner, Henry A. Wallace, Harry S Truman

★ ★ ★

Born:	January 30, 1882; New York
Occupation:	Farmer, Lawyer, Naval Officer, State Senator
Wife:	Eleanor Roosevelt, his fifth cousin, once removed
Children:	Five sons, one daughter
Died:	April 12, 1945
Buried:	Hyde Park, New York

★ ★ ★

Notable facts: Height of the Great Depression; prohibition repealed; Social Security Act passed; national minimum wage introduced; World War II began, U.S. entered after Japanese attack on Pearl Harbor; New Deal implemented.

The only President to serve three terms, during which few knew of his paralysis throughout presidency.

Franklin D. Roosevelt

*The only thing we have to fear
is fear itself.*

---

*These unhappy times call for the
building of plans . . .
from the bottom up.*

Franklin D. Roosevelt

The only limit to our realization of tomorrow will be our doubts of today.

Franklin D. Roosevelt

I have no expectation of making a hit every time I come to bat. What I seek is the highest possible batting average.

DID YOU KNOW?

Franklin Roosevelt almost died at birth. Born blue and unconscious, his life was spared by his doctor's mouth-to-mouth resuscitation.

Franklin Roosevelt was the first President to use the media effectively for his own political purposes. Speaking directly over the radio to "the people," his friendly talks became known as "fireside chats," which had the underlying motive of marshaling wide support for his New Deal federal relief programs.

HARRY S TRUMAN, DEMOCRAT

33rd President: 1945-1953

Vice-Presidents: Edward R. Stettinius, Jr., James F. Byrnes,
George C. Marshall, Alben W. Barkley.

★ ★ ★

Born:	May 8, 1884, Missouri
Occupation:	Senator, Judge
Wife:	Bess Wallace
Children:	One daughter
Died:	December 26, 1972
Buried:	Independence, Missouri

★ ★ ★

Notable facts: Truman Doctrine announced stating U.S. must help free people maintain freedom; atomic bombs dropped; World War II ended; signed United Nations Charter; Nuremberg Trials; nation of Israel established; NATO formed; Korean War started.

Known for spicy conversations, leaving no doubt who was boss. This "little man from Missouri" came to be known as "usually right on the big decisions."

Harry S Truman

If you can't convince them, confuse them!

Everyone deserves an even break.

The "S" in Harry Truman's name is not an abbreviation but is his complete middle name—the result of compromise between his parents disputing over naming him after his paternal grandfather "Shippe" or his maternal grandfather "Solomon."

Harry S Truman

It's the horse that comes in first at the finish that counts.

The buck stops here.

Harry S Truman

*If you can't stand the heat,
get out of the kitchen.*

---

*Never sit on a fence; get on
one side or the other.*

DID YOU KNOW?

A sickly child with bad eyesight, forced into the world of books instead of sports, Harry S Truman became a voracious reader. By the age of fourteen, he had borrowed every book in the town library!

DWIGHT D. EISENHOWER, REPUBLICAN
34th President: 1953-1961
Vice-President: Richard M. Nixon

★ ★ ★

Born: October 14, 1890; Texas
Occupation: Army Five-Star General
Wife: Mary "Mamie" Geneva Doud
Children: Two sons
Died: March 28, 1969
Buried: Abilene, Kansas

★ ★ ★

Notable facts: Korean War ended; Joseph McCarthy's anti-
communist crusade heightened; racial segregation
declared unconstitutional; construction of interstate
highway system; NASA established.

Five-star General; Supreme Commander of Allied
Forces during World War II; voted into office on
political theme, "I like Ike."

DWIGHT D. EISENHOWER

*Accomplishment will prove to be a journey,
not a destination.*

---

*The present situation is to be regarded
as one of opportunity for us
and not of disaster.*

DWIGHT D. EISENHOWER

Weakness cannot cooperate with anything.
Only strength can cooperate.

Assemble all the facts on a problem,
and it often solves itself.

DID YOU KNOW?

Dwight D. Eisenhower's unwavering disciplines included signing an average of 200 documents per day. In addition, he insisted upon having knowledge of every item signed, each signature carrying with it the burden of responsibility.

John "Jack" F. Kennedy, Democrat

35th President: 1961-1963
Vice-President: Lyndon B. Johnson

★ ★ ★

Born: May 29, 1917; Massachusetts
Occupation: Journalist, Naval Officer, Senator
Wife: Jacqueline Bouvier
Children: One son, One daughter
Died: November 22, 1963
Buried: Arlington National Cemetery

★ ★ ★

Notable facts: East Germany closed border between East and West Berlin; Peace Corps created; failed Bay of Pigs invasion; American astronauts explored space; Cuban Missile Crisis; implementation of "The President's counsel on Fitness" into the public-school systems.

First Catholic elected President; a dynamic public speaker, greatly mourned after his assassination in a Dallas, Texas motorcade — often referred to as "the end of Camelot."

John "Jack" F. Kennedy

*Ask not what your country can do for you—
ask what you can do for your country.*

---

*Let us resolve to be masters, not the victims,
of our history—controlling our own destiny
without giving way to blind suspicions
and emotions.*

John "Jack" F. Kennedy

Let us never negotiate out of fear, but let us never fear to negotiate.

Our task . . . is not to fix the blame for the past, but to fix the course for the future.

DID YOU KNOW?

"Jack" Kennedy was the first President born in the twentieth century.

LYNDON B. JOHNSON, DEMOCRAT
36th President: 1963-1969
Vice-President: John William McCormack

★ ★ ★

Born: August 27, 1908; Texas
Occupation: Teacher, Navy Commander, Public Official
Wife: Claudia Taylor "Lady Bird"
Children: Two daughters
Died: January 22, 1973
Buried: L.B.J. Ranch, Texas

★ ★ ★

Notable facts: Vietnam War expanded; Civil Rights Act became
              law; Great Society implemented; medicare and
              medicaid created.

              Skillful at handling Congress, none of his thirty vetoes
              were overridden, unfortunately his term was overshad-
              owed by the controversial Vietnam War policy.

LYNDON B. JOHNSON

*The hardest task is not to do what is right
but to know what is right.*

---

*We must change to
master change.*

LYNDON B. JOHNSON

Our test before us . . . is not whether our commitments match our will and our courage; but whether we have the will and the courage to match our commitments.

In the arsenal of truth, there is no greater weapon than fact.

Lyndon B. Johnson was the last President whose
roots and early experiences would bridge the gap
between the old America of local frontiers, cross-
roads and close neighbors, and the new America of
world power, big cities, and unknown neighbors.
His deepest motivation as a public figure was to
make people neighbors again.

Richard M. Nixon, Republican
37th President: 1969-1974
Vice-Presidents: Spiro T. Agnew, Gerald R. Ford

★ ★ ★

Born:	January 9, 1913; California
Occupation:	Lawyer, Navy Officer, Senator
Wife:	Thelma "Pat" Ryan
Children:	Two daughters
Died:	April 22, 1994

★ ★ ★

Notable facts: American astronauts landed on moon; Vietnam War ended; visited China; Watergate scandal; under threat of impeachment, Nixon resigned, although later pardoned.

Tremendous success internationally through implementation of his foreign policies, a domain which he significantly impacted, even after his term in office.

Richard M. Nixon

Others may hate you but those who hate you don't win unless you hate them.

The ability to be cool, confident, and decisive in crisis . . . is the direct result of how well the individual has prepared himself for battle.

Gerald R. Ford, Republican
38th President: 1974-1977
Vice-President: Nelson Rockefeller

Born:	July 14, 1913; Nebraska
Occupation:	Lawyer, Congressman
Wife:	Elizabeth Bloomer
Children:	Three sons, one daughter

Notable facts: Granted former President Nixon unconditional pardon; U.S. bicentennial; final Communist victory in Southeast Asia.

Only man in American history to hold offices of President and Vice-President without being elected to either office by the American people.

GERALD R. FORD

A government big enough to give you everything you want is a government big enough to take from you everything you have.

It's the quality of the ordinary, the straight, the square, that accounts for . . . great stability.

GERALD R. FORD

Challenge and adversity have given us confidence and experience.

Gerald Ford turned down two professional football contracts, from the Detroit Lions and Green Bay Packers, to study law at Yale. He earned tuition money coaching football.

JAMES "JIMMY" E. CARTER, DEMOCRAT
39th President: 1977-1981
Vice-President: Walter F. Mondale

★ ★ ★

Born:	October 1, 1924; Georgia
Occupation:	Farmer, Engineer, Scientist, Businessman
Wife:	Rosalynn Smith
Children:	Three sons, one daughter

★ ★ ★

Notable facts: Camp David Accords; Canal Zone ceded to Republic of Panama; U.S. official recognition of People's Republic of China; U.S. Embassy personnel taken hostage in Iran; supporting figure for "The Habitat for Humanity"; after term was known as the "Unofficial Goodwill Ambassador" for his gift in foreign policy.

James "Jimmy" E. Carter

We must adjust to changing times and still hold to unchanging principles.

America did not invent human rights. Human rights invented America.

James "Jimmy" E. Carter

A strong nation, like a strong person, can afford to be gentle, firm, thoughtful, and restrained.

When told of his plans to run for President, Jimmy Carter's mother asked: "President of what?"

Ronald Reagan, Republican
40th President: 1981-1989
Vice-President: George Bush

★ ★ ★

Born:	February 6, 1911; Illinois
Occupation:	Actor, Governor
Wives:	Jane Wyman, Nancy Davis
Children:	Two sons, two daughters

★ ★ ★

Notable facts: Appointed Sandra Day O'Connor, first female Justice of U.S. Supreme Court; wounded in assassination attempt; U.S. invasion of Granada; Iran-Contra scandal; thawing of Cold War via talks with communist leader Gorbachev.

Known as the "Teflon" President, because no matter how many mistakes he made, no criticism would stick to him; considered the conservative's conservative.

Ronald Reagan

*America is too great
for small dreams.*

---

*It's time we reduced the
federal budget and left the
family budget alone.*

Ronald Reagan

Many . . . programs come from a good heart, but not all come from a clear head.

Wars begin when governments believe the price of aggression is cheap.

Ronald Reagan, always a punster, began one of his weekly radio broadcasts with: "My fellow Americans, I am pleased to tell you that I've signed legislation that will outlaw Russia forever. We begin bombing in five minutes." Even this "innocent joke" could not dampen public enthusiasm.

GEORGE BUSH, REPUBLICAN
41st President: 1989-1993
Vice-President: J. Danforth Quayle

★ ★ ★

Born:	June 12, 1924; Massachusetts
Occupation:	Fighter pilot, Congressional Post, Permanent Representative to the UN, Director of the CIA
Wife:	Barbara Pierce
Children:	Four sons, one daughter

★ ★ ★

Notable facts: Invasion of Panama; end of Cold War through collapse of Iron Curtain, U.S.S.R. and communism in Eastern Europe; Persian Gulf War (Desert Storm).

Came to presidency with wide experience in both private and public sectors.

GEORGE BUSH

*Strength in the pursuit of peace
is no vice.*

---

*Isolation in the pursuit
of security is no virtue.*

GEORGE BUSH

*Appeasement does
not work.*

---

*I'm President of the United States,
and I'm not going to eat
any more broccoli.*

DID YOU KNOW?

In 1991, Barbara Bush made more income than her husband George, having published *Millie's Book*, an account of life in the White House as experienced by their pet spaniel. The book, which became a best-seller, earned $889,176, which Mrs. Bush donated to charity.

WILLIAM "BILL" CLINTON, DEMOCRAT
42nd President: 1993-present
Vice-President: Albert Gore, Jr.

Born:	August 19, 1946; Arkansas
Occupation:	Law School Professor, Governor
Wife:	Hillary Rodham
Children:	One daughter

Notable facts: NAFTA: North American Free Trade Agreement; passage of Brady handgun bill; civil war in Bosnia; terrorist bombings of New York City's World Trade Center and Oklahoma City federal building.

First postwar, baby-boom-generation President.

WILLIAM "BILL" CLINTON

There can be no "them" in America.
There's only "us."

There is nothing wrong . . . that can't be
fixed with what is right. . . .

William "Bill" Clinton

I like the job—the bad days are part of it.

DID YOU KNOW?

Bill Clinton was a boy scout, sang in the church choir, and formed a jazz combo with two friends in which they performed wearing sunglasses and were known as the "Three Blind Mice."

DID YOU KNOW?

 $\mathbf{B}$ ill Clinton decided on a career in politics in 1963. After having the opportunity to shake hands with President John Kennedy in the White House Rose Garden, he never looked back.

Additional copies of this book and other titles in the
In The Midst of Greatness Series
are available at your local bookstore.

The C.E.O.s' Little Instruction Book

Trade Life Books
Tulsa, Oklahoma